W9-DGP-291

The TOXIC WASTE TIME BOMB

BY JUDITH WOODBURN

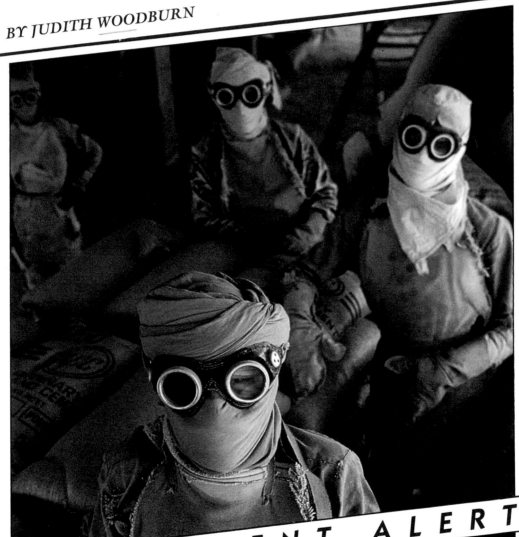

ENVIRONMENT ALERT!

Gareth Stevens Publishing
MILWAUKEE

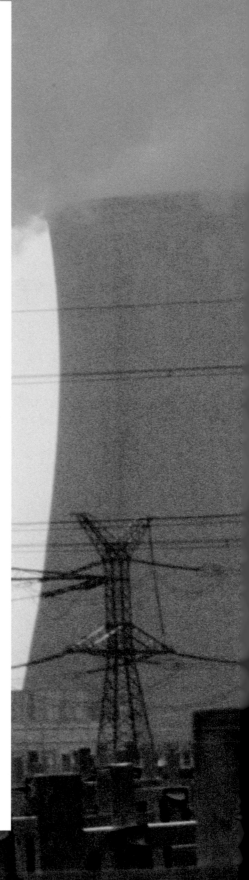

For a free color catalog describing Gareth Stevens' list of high-quality books, call 1-800-341-3569 (USA) or 1-800-461-9120 (Canada).

Library of Congress Cataloging-in-Publication Data

Woodburn, Judith, 1959-
    The toxic waste time bomb / Judith Woodburn.
        p.   cm. — (Environment alert!)
    Includes bibliographical references and index.
    Summary: Discusses the sources, dangers, and disposal of nuclear and toxic wastes.
    ISBN 0-8368-0699-9
    1. Hazardous wastes—Juvenile literature.   2. Industrial accidents—Environmental aspects—
Juvenile literature. 3. Environmental health—Juvenile literature. [1. Hazardous wastes. 2.
Pollution.] I. Title. II. Series.
TD1030.5.W66   1991
363.72'87—dc20   91-50342

Edited, designed, and produced by
Gareth Stevens Publishing
1555 North RiverCenter Drive, Suite 201
Milwaukee, WI 53212, USA

Picture Credits

© Brad Bower/Picture Group, p. 22 (lower); Kurt Carloni/Artisan, 1992, pp. 12-13 (upper), p. 18, p. 25 (lower); © Nicholas De Vore/Bruce Coleman Limited, p. 11 (lower); © Greg Evans International, p. 9; © Greenpeace/Dorreboom, p. 25 (upper); © Greenpeace/Van der Veer, pp. 20-21; Matthew Groshek, 1992, p. 14; © Hewetson/ Greenpeace, p. 15; © Arthur R. Hill/Visuals Unlimited, p. 10; © Leitinger/Greenpeace, pp. 2-3; © L. Linkhart/Visuals Unlimited, p. 8 (lower); © S. Maslowski/Visuals Unlimited, p. 5 (left); Michael Medynsky/Artisan, 1992, p. 8 (upper); Courtesy of New York State Department of Economic Development, p. 11 (upper); © Mickey Osterreicher/Photoreporters, pp. 16-17, p. 17; © Picture Perfect USA, front cover (inset), title; © Pictures Colour Library/Third Coast Stock Source, pp. 4-5; © Recio/ Greenpeace, p. 23; © Larry Roberts/Visuals Unlimited, p. 5 (right); © Science VU/ Visuals Unlimited, cover; © Roger Scruton/IMPACT Photos, pp. 26-27; © Zachary Singer/Greenpeace, p. 21; © W. Eugene Smith/Black Star, p. 13; Tim Spransy, 1991, pp. 28-29; UPI/Bettmann, pp. 12-13 (lower), p. 19 (upper); © 1992 Greg Vaughn, pp. 24-25; Keith Ward, 1992, pp. 6-7; © Joy Wolf/Picture Group, p. 19 (lower); © Christian Zuber/Bruce Coleman Limited, p. 22 (upper).

Map information on pp. 6-7 and 14 from *Atlas of the Environment*, New York: Prentice Hall Press, 1990, pp. 102-103.

Series editor: Patricia Lantier-Sampon
Series designer: Laurie Shock
Book designer: Sabine Beaupré
Picture researcher: Diane Laska
Research editor: David Kent

Printed in the United States of America

1 2 3 4 5 6 7 8 9 97 96 95 94 93 92

At this time, Gareth Stevens, Inc., does not use 100 percent recycled paper, although the paper used in our books does contain about 30 percent recycled fiber. This decision was made after a careful study of current recycling procedures revealed their dubious environmental benefits. We will continue to explore recycling options.

[signature]
President

CONTENTS

Words that appear in the glossary are printed in **boldface** type the first time they appear in the text.

TOXIC WASTE CHAOS
Dangerous Leftovers

Everything we do creates leftovers. Most of these leftovers are harmless, such as grass clippings or banana peels. But some leftovers are poisonous to people and animals. **Sewage** from our houses and chemicals from factories are some of the main sources of **toxic wastes** in the world.

Toxic wastes are a major health threat to the whole planet. But although some people have tried, there is really no way to get rid of poisons forever. When they are dumped into the ocean, the poisons can hurt sea animals or **contaminate** fish that people eat. Poisons that have been buried in the ground seep into the drinking water. And when poisonous substances are handled carelessly, accidents can happen that will endanger whole cities. When people are exposed to toxic wastes, they may develop **cancer**, brain damage, or other problems.

People are creating more and more toxic waste that they can't control. If we don't learn to create less of it and then **dispose** of it properly, our food and water supplies will all be poisoned.

Above: Nuclear power plants create lots of harmless steam. But the real danger posed by nuclear waste — nuclear radiation — is invisible.

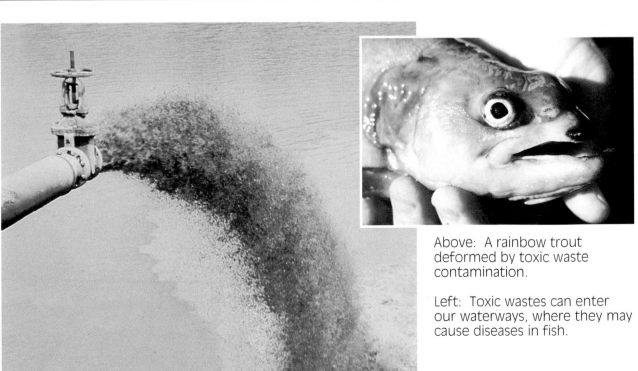

Above: A rainbow trout deformed by toxic waste contamination.

Left: Toxic wastes can enter our waterways, where they may cause diseases in fish.

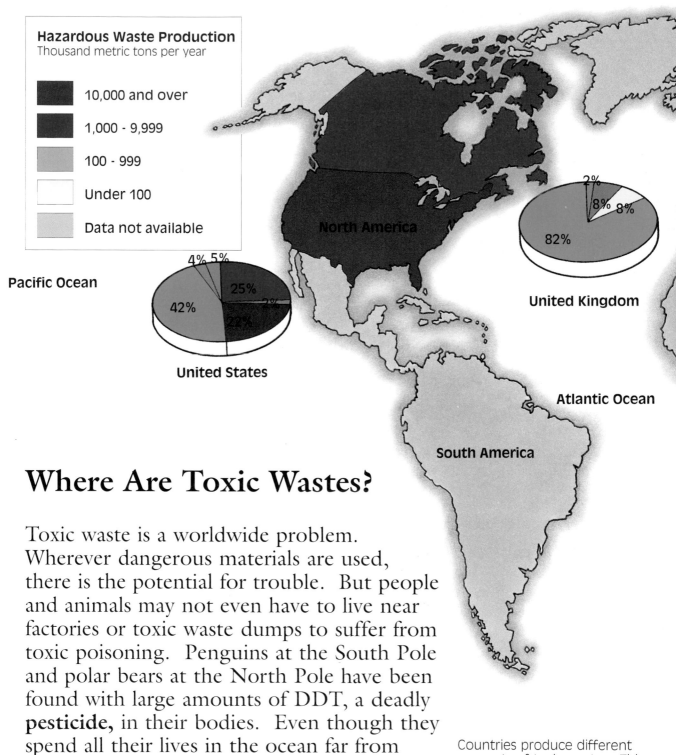

Hazardous Waste Production
Thousand metric tons per year

- 10,000 and over
- 1,000 - 9,999
- 100 - 999
- Under 100
- Data not available

Pacific Ocean

North America

United States

4% 5% 25% 2% 22% 42%

United Kingdom

2% 8% 8% 82%

Atlantic Ocean

South America

Where Are Toxic Wastes?

Toxic waste is a worldwide problem. Wherever dangerous materials are used, there is the potential for trouble. But people and animals may not even have to live near factories or toxic waste dumps to suffer from toxic poisoning. Penguins at the South Pole and polar bears at the North Pole have been found with large amounts of DDT, a deadly **pesticide,** in their bodies. Even though they spend all their lives in the ocean far from factories, many whales and dolphins also have been contaminated with toxic chemicals that were dumped into the sea.

Countries produce different amounts of toxic wastes. This chart shows how much some countries produce and the methods they use to try to dispose of it.

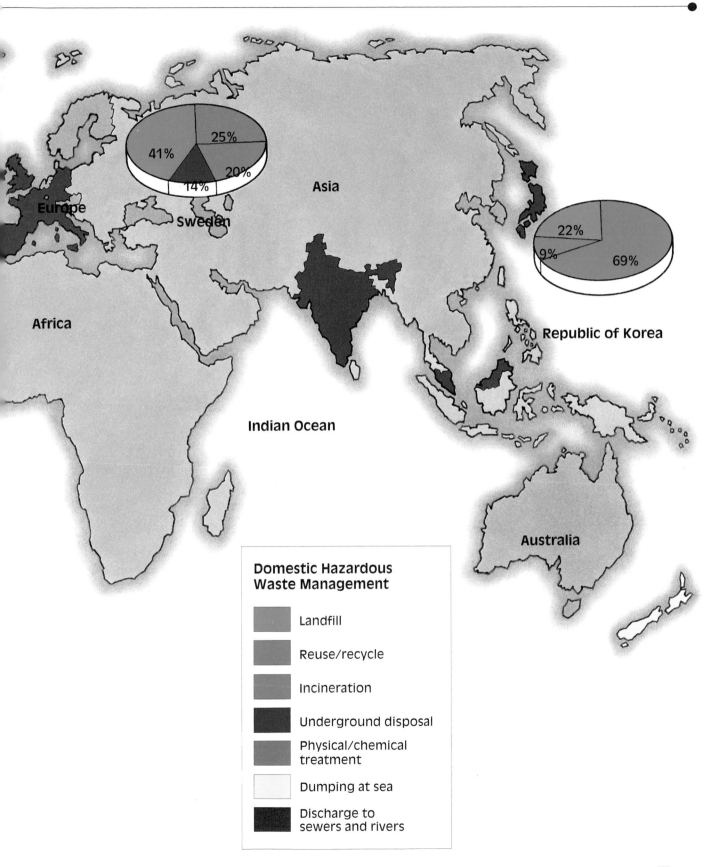

Europe

25%

41%

14%

20%

Sweden

Asia

Africa

22%

9%

69%

Republic of Korea

Indian Ocean

Australia

**Domestic Hazardous
Waste Management**

Landfill

Reuse/recycle

Incineration

Underground disposal

Physical/chemical
treatment

Dumping at sea

Discharge to
sewers and rivers

Many Kinds of Toxic Wastes

More than 70,000 chemicals go into making the products we use every day. At least 500 of these chemicals are known to be toxic. Some, such as DDT and BHC, go into making pesticides. They can cause cancer and can damage growing human and animal babies before they are even born. Another toxic waste, vinyl chloride, is a chemical left over from making plastic. It can damage people's lungs and livers.

Radioactive waste comes from leftover fuel from **nuclear power plants** and leftover materials from bomb factories. Nuclear waste gives off **ionizing radiation**. When people are exposed to this radiation, they may get radiation sickness. Radiation sickness can cause a person to lose hair or teeth, to bleed internally, and sometimes even to die.

Pesticide Alternatives

Many countries around the world now use methods of controlling pests that depend very little on pesticides. For example, Indonesian rice farmers use a system called integrated pest management. This system allows the use of very small amounts of pesticides. The major burden of pest control lies on themselves! Insects like wolf spiders and ladybugs help farmers keep their valuable crops free from the brown planthoppers that destroy rice plants. The system of integrated pest management has not only cut down on the amount of money spent on chemical pesticides; it has also resulted in higher plant yields for the farmers.

Left: A California farmer sprays his apple orchard with insecticide.

Right: Workers in protective clothing mix chemicals inside a factory.

The Dioxin Threat

The Hyde Park toxic waste dump near the Niagara River in New York State is the world's largest source of dioxin contamination — a disaster just waiting to happen. More than 70,000 tons of chemical wastes were buried there before 1975. But they didn't stay buried. Now, the dioxins are leaking into the Niagara River. Scientists are very concerned because one shovelful of chemicals from the Hyde Park dump would be enough to kill most of the animals in nearby Lake Ontario!

Dioxins are some of the most powerful toxic wastes of all. They are poisonous in extremely tiny amounts — one part per billion. In other words, you could **dilute** one drop of dioxin with more than 13,000 gallons (49,200 L) of water, and it still would be dangerous.

Dioxins are a family of chemicals found in weed killers, bleached paper, and other sources. Dioxins can also be created when toxic waste is **incinerated.** The dioxins come out of the smokestack and go into the air. When people are exposed to dioxins, they can develop a painful skin disease. Animals exposed to dioxin become thinner and thinner until they die.

Opposite: A chemical waste incineration plant.

Right: A paper mill in Newfoundland.

How Toxic Wastes Get into the Earth and Water

Before people understood how dangerous toxic waste was, they just got rid of it the easiest way: they buried it in the soil or just pumped it into the nearest river or lake. Eventually, however, people who lived near the toxic dumps became sick. They began protesting the careless way companies were disposing of their toxic garbage.

Now, we have special **landfills** for toxic wastes. These landfills are specially constructed with clay and plastic liners to keep the toxins from leaking out. But often, the chemicals leak out anyway.

The toxins can soak into the earth around the dump. Sometimes animals eat plants that have absorbed the poisons, and then people eat the animals. Or the poisons slowly trickle into the water supply. Even water treatment plants can't get rid of all the poisons in the water.

landfill

Right: Fish caught off the coast of Japan are poisoned with mercury and not fit to eat.

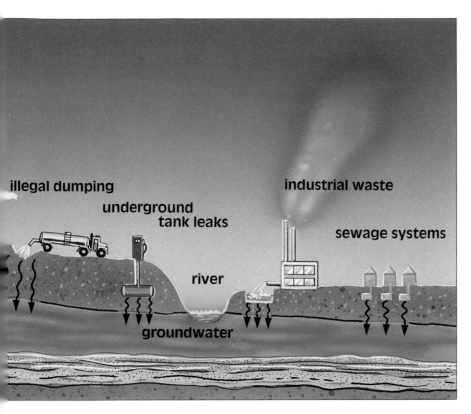

Left: This drawing shows some of the many ways that toxic waste can contaminate the soil and our fresh water supplies.

illegal dumping

underground tank leaks

industrial waste

sewage systems

river

groundwater

The Poisoned Waters of Minimata Bay

For years, the CHISSO chemical factory in Minimata, Japan, dumped its toxic garbage into the sea. But about 35 years ago, strange things started happening. All the cats in the village died. People couldn't stop shaking. They shouted. Some went blind, or, like the young woman being held in her mother's arms above, suffered severe brain damage. It took scientists years to figure out that the factory was dumping **mercury** into the ocean. Mercury is poisonous even in tiny amounts. As oysters on the nearby ocean bottom grew, the mercury became concentrated in them. When people (and cats) ate the oysters, mercury built up in their bodies, too. About 800 people have died from mercury poisoning in Minimata.

The Midnight Dumpers

Some people do not want to follow the rules for disposing of toxic waste safely. They think it is too expensive. So they resort to sneaky ways of getting rid of it. They are called "midnight dumpers" because they often sneak around late at night, dumping huge truckloads of chemicals into public sewers, or into landfills that aren't set up to contain toxic waste. Sometimes they even dump toxic waste into the basements of empty buildings! One midnight dumper was recently caught in the United States. He had to go to jail for two years and pay millions of dollars in fines.

Below: Some countries pay other countries to take toxic waste off their hands. This chart shows how much toxic waste is exported by several wealthy nations to other nations. The numbers show thousands of metric tons.

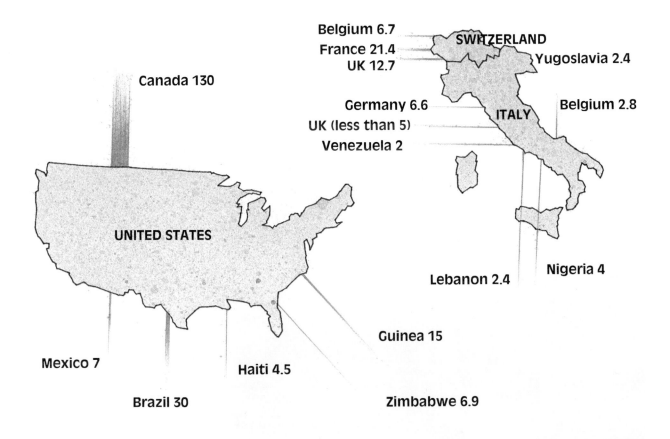

Belgium 6.7
France 21.4
UK 12.7

SWITZERLAND

Yugoslavia 2.4

Canada 130

Germany 6.6
UK (less than 5)
Venezuela 2

ITALY

Belgium 2.8

UNITED STATES

Nigeria 4

Lebanon 2.4

Mexico 7

Guinea 15

Haiti 4.5

Brazil 30

Zimbabwe 6.9

Companies in wealthy countries like the United States, Italy, and France also try to get rid of toxic waste by paying poorer countries to take it. Many countries, such as Nigeria, get angry when other countries use their lands as dumping grounds. But in other lands, such as eastern Germany (once a separate country), leaders have been so desperate for money that they took the wastes, even though they had no way to dispose of them safely.

Above: A ship dumps waste off the coast of Australia.

FACT FILE
The Disaster at Love Canal

Love Canal is a 3,000-foot (915-m) -long canal near Niagara Falls in the state of New York. For ten years, the Hooker Chemical company dumped its poisonous garbage into Love Canal. Then, in 1953, the company gave some land nearby to the community for a new school.

This seemed like a nice thing for the company to do. But as the years passed, the chemicals started leaking. Children at the school got severe burns on their hands and feet from playing in contaminated areas. The chemicals leaked into people's basements. Many people got sick. Eventually, the school had to be closed, and a thousand families had to move away from the canal. To this day, no one lives there.

Some leaders are trying to convince people that Love Canal is safe enough to live near again. To help people forget about the problems of Love Canal, the government has changed the area's name to Black Creek Village. But many people do not want to forget. They say that no one will ever be able to live near Love Canal again.

Right: Pumps are used to suck toxic chemicals from underground near Love Canal.

Below: Houses are boarded up and the school playground has been plowed under at Love Canal.

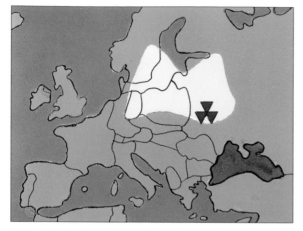

April 29, 1986

April 30, 1986

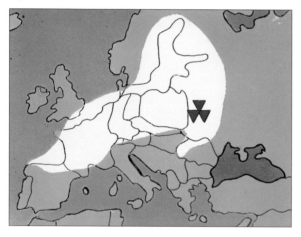

May 1, 1986

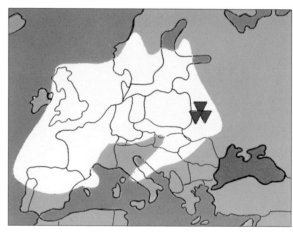

May 2, 1986

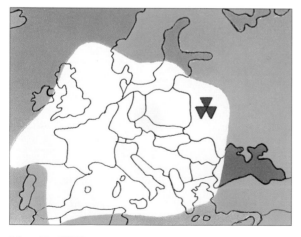

May 3, 1986

In 1986, an explosion at the Chernobyl nuclear power station in the former Soviet Union created a cloud of toxic radiation (shown in yellow) that quickly spread over most of Europe. Twenty-nine people died as a direct result of radiation poisoning, and many more were contaminated by radiation carried by the wind. The effects of this explosion on the environment were very severe.

Toxic Accidents

Sometimes, dangerous materials get into the soil, air, and water. In 1986, a deadly accident occurred at the Chernobyl nuclear power plant in the Soviet Union. The radioactive fuel got too hot and exploded, exposing people living near the nuclear reactor to radiation. Within a month, 29 people died of radiation poisoning.

Chemical accidents can be just as dangerous as nuclear accidents. In 1984, a tank of **methyl isocyanate** gas overheated at the Union Carbide pesticide factory in Bhopal, India. A plume of deadly gas escaped into the air, and people couldn't run fast enough to escape the fumes. By the next day, 3,000 people had died from breathing toxic fumes.

Deadly accidents like these don't happen very often. To prevent accidents from occurring, we need to have stricter rules for factories that use toxic materials.

The Dioxin Tragedy

Dioxin is one of the most toxic of all artificial substances. It is used in many herbicides and is one of the main ingredients in Agent Orange, a chemical spray used in the Vietnam War by the United States. In 1976, a major explosion occurred at the Icmesa chemical factory in Seveso, Italy. This major industrial accident released large quantities of dioxin into the air, killing huge numbers of animals, such as the sheep pictured above. A total of 730 families were forced to evacuate the area because of dioxin poisoning.

Left: Two victims of the Bhopal chemical disaster.

CLEANING UP THE TOXIC MESS
Defusing the Toxic Time Bomb

All over the world, people have started to clean up some of the toxic messes. In the United States, a program called Superfund was started to help pay for cleaning up toxic dumps. At Love Canal, scientists are burning the waste with special torches that burn at 10,000°F (5,537°C). The torches are so hot that they may be able to transform the toxic chemicals into safe materials.

In Europe, the United Nations' Regional Seas Programme is cleaning up toxic pollution in the Mediterranean Sea. People are working to keep toxic dumps from even getting started, and conservationists throughout the continent have successfully prevented new toxic dumps from opening. There is also a new international treaty that will keep countries from using other lands as toxic dumps.

One exciting way of dealing with toxic wastes is to use them for something else. In Europe and the United States, scientists have been experimenting with using toxic ash from incinerators to create bricks. In New York, they are building an 8,000-square-foot (743-sq-m) building with these special bricks. Elsewhere, scientists are using incinerator ash to create a special material for paving roads. They call this special material "ash-phalt."

Above: People protesting the incineration of toxic wastes at sea.

Right: Family members protest a toxic waste incinerator in their community.

Safely Storing Radioactive Waste

Figuring out what to do with nuclear waste is really tricky. That's because it stays dangerous for thousands of years, and it's hard to think of any place that will hold it safely for that long. If we bury nuclear waste in the ground, an earthquake might cause a leak. If we put it in the ocean, the saltwater could eat away at the container.

Some scientists think the best way to deal with radioactive waste is to surround small pieces of it with a very thick, strong kind of glass and bury it very deep in the Earth. But other people think there is just no way to safely store nuclear waste long enough. In Germany and many other countries, protestors are stopping companies from using nuclear material to generate electricity or to make bombs. This helps to reduce the production of radioactive waste.

Radioactive Beagles

Decades ago, the United States government tested the effects of nuclear weapons by exposing dozens of beagles to nuclear radiation. When the dogs died, however, there was a problem. Because they had been exposed to radiation, the bodies of the dogs were toxic waste, and so were all the dogs' droppings! The researchers decided to store the dangerous wastes carefully in a building until they could figure out what to do with them. As this book was being written, the experimenters still had not found a way to permanently dispose of the radioactive dogs.

Left: A train carries incinerated ash and scrap to a landfill for disposal.

A landfill in Almaden, Spain, where mercury waste from several countries is dumped.

Targeting the Toxins in Your Home

Factories aren't the only sources of toxic waste. About 25 percent of toxic waste comes from people's homes. We create toxic waste right in our own homes every time we use products like bleach and scouring powder or get rid of things like motor oil, old cans of paint, and weed killers. The average house has between 3 and 8.5 gallons (11 to 38 L) of toxic waste!

By disposing of them properly, we can make sure these toxins don't get into our soil and water. Don't just throw toxic products into the trash or down the drain. And never handle these products without a grown-up to help you. Call your local government or the company that makes the product to find out how to dispose of your hazardous waste safely and properly.

Better still, you and your family can switch to nontoxic, homemade products to keep your house clean. You'll find some ideas on page 30.

Above and opposite, above: Old paint cans and batteries are collected for proper disposal.

Opposite, below: Many household products are sources of toxic waste if they are not disposed of correctly.

The Pollution Solution

Now that scientists know just how dangerous some chemicals are, they are working to find safer ways of getting rid of them. One way might be to breed special bacteria that will eat the chemicals. What a lunch!

Another idea is to drill holes miles into the Earth, then shoot the toxic wastes into them. Other people think the best way to get rid of toxic wastes is to burn them in incinerators.

All of these methods, however, could just create new problems. Incinerators, for example, create toxic smoke that pollutes the air. So the best way to handle toxic materials is not to use them in the first place. At home, we can stop using toxic products. But most toxic wastes come from industry, so companies must learn to use fewer toxic chemicals, too. By working together, we can clean up the world's toxic messes — and stop making new ones, too.

Right: An incinerator ship pollutes the air and ruins the natural beauty of this ocean scene.

RESEARCH ACTIVITIES

1. Find out where your water comes from. Does it come from your family's own well or from a city water supply? Call the waterworks in your local government and ask where the city's water comes from. Ask what is done to this water to make it safe to drink.

2. Find out about the factories near your home. What do they make? What kinds of wastes do they produce? How do they dispose of them?

3. Take an inventory of possible toxic substances in your home.   Toxic household materials include weed killer, bug sprays, chlorine bleach, mothballs, oil-based paint and paint thinner, wood preservatives, and batteries. **Note: Do not handle any of these materials without an adult's supervision**.   How many gallons of toxic wastes do you think you have in your home? What could your family do without?

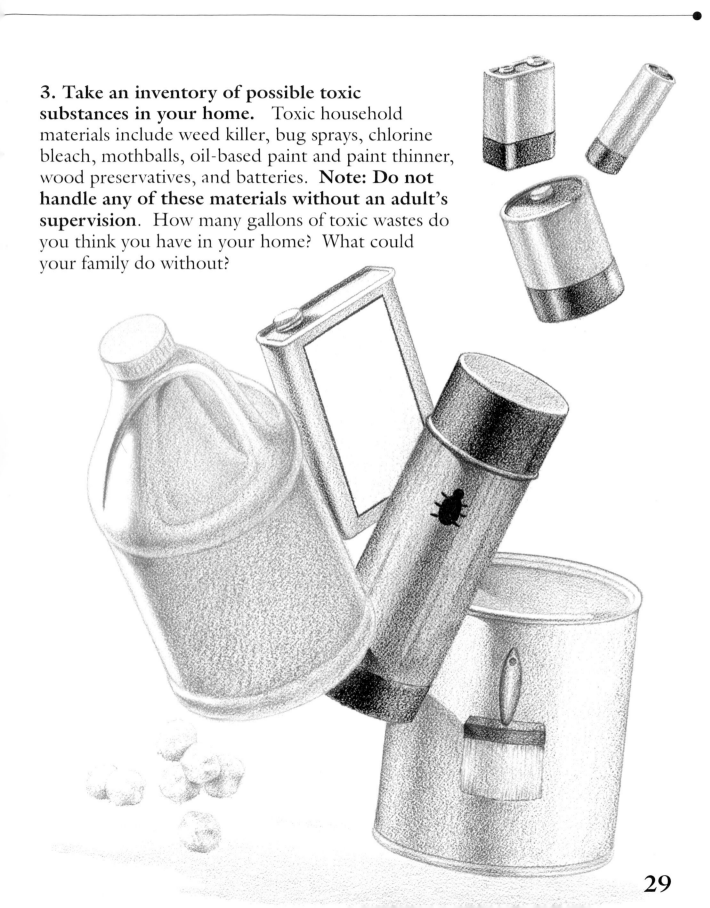

Things You Can Do to Help

1. **Clean up your own act first!** Use nontoxic cleaners when you help around the house. Instead of store-bought scouring powder, which often contains toxic chlorine, use salt or baking soda instead. Instead of store-bought glass cleaner, try mixing one-quarter cup (50 mL) of white vinegar with one cup (250 mL) of water. These homemade cleaners are safer and will save your family money, too.

2. **Think carefully before you buy.** Just about everything we buy in stores — especially plastic products or toys that use batteries — is made in factories that create toxic wastes. The less you buy, the less waste these factories will produce. Instead, try making your own toys out of wood, clay, or paper.

3. **Write to your local government leaders.** Ask them to start an annual household toxic waste collection day if your city doesn't already have one. This way, people won't have to dump dangerous chemicals down the drain.

Places to Write for More Information

Here are some organizations that can give you more information about toxic waste. When you write to them, be sure to tell them exactly what you want to know, and include an envelope with a stamp and your address so they can write back to you.

Citizens' Clearinghouse
   for Hazardous Wastes
P.O. Box 926
Arlington, Virginia 22216

Greenpeace (Canada)
2623 West 4th Avenue
Vancouver, British
   Columbia V6K 1P8

Greenpeace USA
1436 U Street NW
Washington, D.C.
   20009

More Books to Read

Ecology and Conservation, by Steven Seidenberg (Gareth Stevens)
50 Simple Things Kids Can Do to Save the Earth (Earthworks Press)
Managing Toxic Wastes, by Michael Kronenwetter (Messner)
Waste and Recycling, by Barbara James (Steck-Vaughn)

Glossary

cancer — a disease in which certain cells of the body grow out of control, forming tumors or spreading to new parts of the body.

contaminate — to make something impure by adding a substance that doesn't belong there.

dilute — to add water or another liquid to weaken the strength of a substance.

dioxins — a highly toxic family of chemicals used to make poisonous substances such as weed killers and bleaching products.

dispose — to throw away.

incinerate — to burn to ashes.

ionizing radiation — the emission of rays from nuclear materials.

landfills — specially designed places where garbage is disposed of. Landfills often have plastic or clay linings that help stop toxic materials from leaking out.

mercury — a poisonous metal that is in liquid form at ordinary temperatures. Mercury is often used in scientific instruments.

methyl isocyanate — a deadly gas used in the production of some pesticides.

nuclear power plants — places where nuclear fuel is used to generate electricity.

pesticide — a chemical used to kill insects or rodents.

radioactive — any substance that gives off ionizing radiation.

sewage — human wastes that are flushed away with water in sewers or drains.

toxic wastes — poisonous wastes produced during manufacturing and other industrial production processes.

Index